Venice

Texts by
Alessandra Morgagni

Photographs by
Graziano Arici

Contents

Plan of the city on page 110

The Grand Canal

The Grand Canal is the principal waterway of Venice. Two and a half miles long and in some points more than fifteen feet deep, it probably originated as a natural canal, one of the many riverbeds that once flowed into the lagoon, which was continually being dug out and reinforced along its embankments in the past.

This broad canal in the shape of an inverted "S" which divides the city into two parts starts at the Santa Lucia Station and flows into the Bacino (or Basin) di San Marco. The Grand Canal is crossed by three bridges only: the Bridge of the Scalzi in front of the station, the Rialto Bridge, and the wooden Accademia Bridge. Of these, only the Rialto Bridge has ancient origins; the others were built in the last century. It is possible, however, to cross the Canal at other points thanks to a gondola service that ferries passengers from one shore to the other.

Besides being a source of changing water for the streams and canals that flow into it, the Canal is the city's main commercial artery. Boats transporting goods, water-buses filled with tourists and Venetians moving around the city, and gondolas, they all ply along the Grand Canal. Unfortunately the wave motion created by this traffic continually jeopardizes the buildings built alongside it. As someone once said, the Grand Canal is really "the most beautiful street in the world." Magnificent palaces, churches, and public buildings dating from different eras look onto the canal. To move along it at sunset as the lights of the palaces go on makes for one of the most beautiful and memorable moments in a visit to Venice.

Aerial view of the Grand Canal.

Following page
The Grand Canal on a foggy day.

6

The Beginning of the Grand Canal

The **Ponte degli Scalzi** and the Cannaregio Canal characterize the initial part of the Grand Canal. This was an important junction of the city before Venice was connected to land and the automobile terminal at Piazzale Roma was constructed since all the passengers and goods arriving by sea from the mainland entered Venice here. At the corner of the Cannaregio Canal and the Grand Canal, and set back slightly from them, is the 18th century **Palazzo Labia**, now RAI headquarters, but once owned by rich merchants, the Labia family. The part of the palace reflected in the water is actually the back of the building, because its entrance is on Campo San Geremia. Nonetheless it is richly decorated because of its key location. The rooms of the palace are sumptuous and were frescoed by an artist who was the most famous in Venice at that time, Giambattista Tiepolo.

The **Church of San Marcuola** stands on a square which opens onto the Grand Canal. Its construction started in the beginning of the 18th century; however, only the portal and the base of the facade were completed, the rest has a brick finish.

View of the Grand Canal with the Ponte degli Scalzi.

Fondaco dei Turchi.

Church of San Marcuola.

Right
Palazzo Labia.

From the Fondaco dei Turchi to Ca' Pesaro

In front of the Church of San Marcuola is the **Fondaco dei Turchi.** "Fondaco" is synonymous with warehouse, and the building takes its name from the Turks who bought it in order to use it as such: its broad colonnade allowed boats to load and unload goods easily.

Actually, this building dates back to the 13th century and at the time of its construction it was one of the most magnificent buildings on the Grand Canal. It currently is the location of the Museum of Natural History. On the other side of the Grand Canal, is the majestic and imposing **Ca' Vendramin Calergi** by the architect Mauro Codussi which was completed in the first part of the Cinquecento. The composer Richard Wagner lived and died here in 1883; today it functions as the gambling casino during the winter season.

The **Church of San Stae**, with its white facade set back from the Canal, often holds concerts of classical music.

Ca' Pesaro, a masterpiece of the Venetian Baroque by Baldassarre Longhena, houses the Museums of Oriental Art and Modern Art.

Ca' Pesaro.

Gustav Klimt, Salome (detail). Ca' Pesaro.

Ca' Vendramin Calergi (the winter gambling casino).

9

GONDOLAS AND GONDOLIERS

Gondolas are one of the distinct features of the Grand Canal. Once, every patrician family owned one and had a private gondolier in its employ. Today, gondolas are only one of the many tourist attractions the city has to offer. There are many wooden huts on the Grand Canal where gondolas are moored: these are the "stazi" or stopping places where the gondoliers, wearing their traditional striped shirts and straw hats with colored ribbons, rest and wait for their turn to work. In the past, gondolas were not completely open as they are now but were covered by a small barrel-shaped cabin called "felze" which sheltered the passengers from the bad weather especially in the winter months and, at the same time, protected them from prying eyes.

A gondola service ferries between the two shores of the Grand Canal.

Gondola with a "felze."

Vittore Carpaccio, The Miracle of the Cross. Gallerie dell'Accademia.

A gondolier.

Ca' d'Oro

One of the most famous palaces of Venice the **Ca' d'Oro**, which overlooks the Grand Canal, owes its name to its once decorated Gothic style facade.

The roof crenellation, the openwork tracery of the loggias, and the play of voids and solids make the Ca' d'Oro one of the most splendid examples of the Venetian florid Gothic style. It has recently returned to its ancient splendor, thanks to an intelligent job of restoration.

The Ca' d'Oro houses the **Giorgio Franchetti Gallery**, which takes its name from the owner of the palace and the painting collection which he donated to the Italian State at the beginning of the century.

Ca' d'Oro.

Left
*Andrea Mantegna,
St. Sebastian.
Ca' d'Oro,
Franchetti Gallery.*

Right
*Vittore Carpaccio,
The Annunciation
(detail). Franchetti
Gallery.*

The Market Area

The market area, with its wide colonnade, was built in the early part of this century; it houses the picturesque fish market which opens every morning as it always has since 1300.

In front of the market, on the other side of the Canal, is one of the oldest palaces of the city, **Ca' da Mosto**, dating back to the Venetian Byzantine period. This palace was very popular with the foreign writers and artists who visited Venice in the Settecento when it was a famous hotel. In front of Ca' da Mosto are the **Fabbriche Nuove**, a long building designed by Jacopo Sansovino in the middle of the 1500s, now as before the seat of judiciary offices. Its name, the New Buildings, distinguishes it from the **Fabbriche Vecchie** (Old Buildings), the recessed edifice next to it, built a few years before.

Just before the Rialto Bridge, is the ancient **Fondaco dei Tedeschi** where German merchants once plied their trade. Of particular interest is the huge courtyard inside the building which is flanked by three orders of loggias with ogival arches.

Sunset on the Grand Canal.

Ca' Da Mosto.

Above, left
Loggia of the fish market.

Above, right
Fondaco dei Tedeschi.

The Rialto Bridge

The **Rialto Bridge** is undoubtedly one of the symbols of Venice. Its position is strategic for the city since it connects the San Marco part of the city with the commercial zone. The only bridge crossing the canal up to the 19th century, it was originally wooden, as we can see in a painting by Vittore Carpaccio, *The Miracle of the Cross*, at the Gallerie dell'Accademia. Today's bridge was built by Antonio Da Ponte at the end of the 16th century after a competition was held in which other great architects of the time, such as Sansovino, Michelangelo and Palladio, participated. The height of the bridge posed many problems for the builders because of the surrounding swampy terrain. It had to be high enough for the galleys to pass underneath so that they could unload their goods at the markets and warehouses lining the Grand Canal. The bridge was therefore constructed with one powerful arch and is crossed by three pedestrian walks.

A series of elegant palaces line the Grand Canal. Among these are **Palazzo Loredan** and **Ca' Farsetti**, the City Hall of Venice since the early 19th century. Built in the Venetian Byzantine style, the palaces have the typical ground floor arcades where boats could load and unload merchandise. **Palazzo Pisani Moretta** is notable for its rose-colored facade in florid Gothic style with two orders of loggias and openwork.

Palazo Loredan and Ca' Farsetti.

Palazzo Pisani Moretta.

The Rialto Bridge.

From Ca' Foscari to the Bacino di San Marco

At the corner of the Rio Novo which flows into the Grand Canal is the imposing Palazzo Balbi, built at the end of the 16th century and now the headquarters of the Region of the Veneto. Right after the rio is **Ca' Foscari**, the main seat of the University of Venice. It is probably one of the most important buildings on the Grand Canal with its splendid facade decorated with marbles, tracery, and loggias, and is one of the most interesting examples of the Venetian Gothic.

Ca' Rezzonico and **Palazzo Grassi**, both prestigious museum sites, face one another on either side of the Canal. The Baroque Ca' Rezzonico houses the Museum of the Venetian Settecento and has rooms frescoed by Tiepolo. Palazzo Grassi, owned by the FIAT group, was recently restored in order to host high-level temporary exhibitions.

Beside the wooden **Accademia Bridge**, from which we can see the Bacino di San Marco, are the **Gallerie dell'Accademia**, one of the most important museums in the world. As we cross the bridge, to the left is **Palazzo Barbaro**, where the American writer Henry James stayed at various times at the turn of the century and which provided inspiration for the Venetian scenes of his great novel, *The Wings of the Dove*.

The **Casetta delle Rose**, which is set back from the other buildings, is famous because Gabriele D'Annunzio lived there and because the sculptor Antonio Canova had his studio there in the 18th century. Facing it is the 18th century **Ca' Venier dei Leoni**, the ground floor of which has remained unfinished. It houses the Peggy Guggenheim Collection, one of the most important collections of contemporary art, and is where the great American collector lived and died. **Ca' Dario** follows with its characteristic chimneys and polychrome marble decorations on its facade. It is said that whoever lives in this palace will come to no good end.

14

Palazzo Balbi.

Ca' Foscari, seat of the University, and (below) *Palazzo Grassi.*

The Accademia Bridge.

Ca' Dario.

Palazzo Venier dei Leoni, location of the Peggy Guggenheim Collection.

15

The Basilica della Salute

The majestic **Basilica della Salute**, Baldassarre Longhena's Baroque masterpiece, built to commemorate the end of the plague in 1630 stands in the basin near the beginning of the Grand Canal. The church, built on an octagonal plan, is reached by a polygonal stairway that wraps around the facade.

The **Feast of the Madonna della Salute**, an important religious festival fulfilling a vow made during a plague epidemic, is celebrated here. Since 1630 every year on November 21 a bridge of boats is built across the Grand Canal so that Venetians can make a pilgrimage to the Madonna and light their holy candles.

The **Punta della Dogana** is where the Grand Canal flows into the Bacino di San Marco. The reflection of the buildings of Piazza San Marco in the water is an unforgettable sight: the Zecca (Mint), the columns of the Piazzetta, the Doge's Palace, with the Campanile in the background. On top of the Customhouse, where goods coming by sea are entered and cleared, is a statue of Fortune, standing on a golden globe, the world, that serves as a weathervane.

View of the Grand Canal with the domes of the Basilica della Salute in the background.

Feast of the Madonna della Salute.

Punta della Dogana.

Following page
Basilica della Salute.

16

The Island of San Giorgio Maggiore and the Bacino di San Marco

As an integral part of the view onto the Bacino di San Marco, the **island of San Giorgio Maggiore** has inspired artists throughout the centuries.

The majestic and classical **Basilica of San Giorgio** is one of the most beautiful and famous works of Andrea Palladio. Building started in 1566 and terminated twenty-five years later when the great architect was already dead. The grandiose interior of the church conserves such wonderful masterpieces by Tintoretto as his famous *Last Supper* and the *Gathering of the Manna*. The entrance to the campanile is inside the church, and it is well worth going to the top for one of the best views of Venice, the lagoon and the other islands.

Next to the church is a Benedictine monastery which was founded in the 10th century. However, the actual building was started in the 16th century and finished in the 17th. There are two lovely cloisters and a refectory which was designed by Andrea Palladio. The splendid library and its staircase were designed by Baldassarre Longhena. The convent is the seat of the **Fondazione Giorgio Cini**, an important international cultural institution and is often the venue for world conferences and cultural events.

The island of San Giorgio Maggiore.

An evocative image of the Bacino di San Marco with the island of San Giorgio and the Giudecca in the background.

*Following page, below
Aerial view of the Bacino di San Marco.*

18

Two images of the Fondazione Cini: opposite, *one of the cloisters and,* below, *the library.*

Jacopo Tintoretto, Last Supper. Basilica of San Giorgio Maggiore.

THE HISTORICAL REGATTA

Venice is a city of great seafaring traditions and as a consequence many of her festivals are linked to the sea. The most important of these is the **Historical Regatta**, which is held on the first Sunday of September and celebrates all the regattas that have taken place in Venice starting from the first one in the 13th century. A procession garbed in magnificent attire proceeds in gondolas down the Grand Canal whose palaces windows are decorated with banners. The starting point for the different boats participating in the regatta is at the Bacino di San Marco. From there, they proceed to a "paleto" or pole in front the railway station which they have to row around, and then head back to the finishing post near Ca' Foscari. The procession that takes place before the actual races begin recalls the festivities held in Venice at the time of the arrival of Caterina Cornaro, Queen of Cyprus. A parade of boats, called "bissone," with their oarsmen in period costumes, proceeds along the Canal with the Doge saluting the crowd from one of them. One regatta follows another during the course of the day, but the most popular is that of the "gondolini," small swift gondolas manned by two rowers.

Another wonderful sea festival is the **Regatta of the Maritime Republics** which is held in memory of the ancient maritime glory of four cities: Venice, Amalfi, Pisa and Genoa. This takes place every four years in Venice and in the other cities during the other years. Before the actual regatta the representatives of the cities which were once the maritime republics, attired in traditional costumes, parade around Piazza San Marco.

Yet another marine festival is the **Vogalonga** (the Long Row) which takes place on the first Sunday of May. This is a very popular event since any Venetian who can handle an oar can participate. It is not a competitive race and includes boats and oars of all sizes and shapes. The regatta itself takes place not only on the Grand Canal but also around the islands and islets of the northern lagoon. It is a wonderful sight to see all the boats in the Bacino di San Marco before they start off.

This page,
from top to bottom
The Historical Regatta, two moments of the Regatta of the Maritime Republics and the Vogalonga.

Following page
The parade of boats during the Historical Regatta.

Piazza San Marco

Piazza San Marco is the heart of Venice. Visited every year by millions of tourists, it contains the most famous buildings of the city: the Basilica of San Marco, the Doge's Palace, the Campanile, the Procuratie, the Biblioteca Marciana. Because of its importance, it is the only large open space in the city that takes the name "piazza." All the others, according to their sizes, are either "campi" or "campielli." Countless artists have immortalized views of the piazza and its monuments on their canvases; the festivities celebrated there have been described, the people who have frequented the piazza portrayed, and it has provided a setting for many a story and novel. More than one writer has called it "the most beautiful drawing room in the world." The monuments surrounding it bear witness to the past glory and rich history and art of the city and each of them represents a particular period of that past. Throughout the centuries the piazza has been the religious, political and social heart of the city and consequently, the theater of all its great events: the return from a naval victory, the arrival of a king or ambassador from afar, a religious ceremony, Carnival. Even now Piazza San Marco is often the theater of great events.

The way Piazza San Marco looks today is the result of a long series of changes which in its more important aspects terminated only in the last century.

Piazza San Marco.

*Gentile Bellini,
Procession in
Piazza San Marco.
Gallerie
dell'Accademia.*

The Campanile of St. Mark

From the top of the **Campanile** (bell tower) **of St. Mark** there is a stupendous view of the Piazza and the city.

In 1902 the campanile suddenly collapsed, but it was rebuilt exactly as it was. The loggia at the base of the bell tower was designed by Jacopo Sansovino and marks the beginning of the Piazzetta, that is, the area in front of the lagoon.

Canaletto, Piazza San Marco. New York, private collection.

The Campanile and Basilica of San Marco reflected in a shop window.

View of the Campanile from the Doge's Palace.

Performance in Piazza San Marco.

Following page View of the Basilica of San Marco and the Clock Tower at night.

The Procuratie Vecchie and the Clock Tower

On Piazza San Marco are located the Old and New Procuratie, two long arcaded buildings that surround the north and south sides of the Piazza. These buildings open out to the city's most beautiful shops. The **Procuratie Vecchie**, which terminate at the Clock Tower, originally date from the 12th century, but were rebuilt at the beginning of the Cinquecento. The Procurators of St Mark, the highest officials after the doge and established in the year 1000 in order to supervise the construction and conservation of the basilica, had their residences here. This institution, obviously with different powers, still exists today.

Next to the Procuratorie Vecchie is the **Clock Tower**, built at the end of the Quattrocento. On its upper terrace two bronze statues, the *Moors*, strike the hours. Below, the hours and minutes are marked by two small windows. Between these and the *Moors* the symbol of Venice stands out: the *Winged Lion* on a starry blue field. During Ascension week, the figures of the *Wise Men* which are inside the clock emerge every hour from a small side door and kneel before the *Madonna and Child* in the niche.

A foreshortened view of the Piazza from one of the Moors on the Clock Tower.

Following page
The Lion of St. Mark on the Clock Tower.

The dial of the Clock Tower.

The parade of the Wise Men on the Clock Tower.

The Procuratie Vecchie and Nuove come together in the **Napoleonic Wing** on the short side of the Piazza. In order to build this section at the beginning of the 19th century under Napoleon's dominion, the ancient church of San Geminiano was destroyed. The Napoleonic Wing and some rooms of the Procuratie Nuove now house the Museo Correr which possesses the historical and artistic collections of the City of Venice.

The Neoclassical Rooms conserve a splendid collection of statues and bas-reliefs by the sculptor Antonio Canova while the gallery contains famous Venetian paintings, among which Vittore Carpaccio's *Two Venetian Noblewomen*, better known by the title of *Courtesans*.

The Napoleonic Wing, seat of the Museo Correr.

Access staircase of the Museo Correr.

Pieter Bruegel the Younger, Adoration of the Magi.

Paolo Veneziano, St. Augustine, St. Peter, St. John the Baptist, St. John the Evangelist, St. Paul St. George.

Antonio Canova,
Daedalus and
Icarus.

Vittore Carpaccio,
Two Venetian
Noblewomen.

Below
Antonio
da Messina, Pietà
with Three Angels.

Giovanni Bellini,
Crucifixion.

The Procuratie Nuove

On the southern side of the Piazza are the **Procuratie Nuove**; they are "new" because they were built later, and finished in the middle of the Seicento, by Baldassarre Longhena. During the Napoleonic period the whole complex was used as the royal palace.

In the arcades of the Procuratorie Nuove is the Caffè Florian, the famous meeting place frequented by men of letters and travellers during the last century.

The Procuratie Nuove.

Two images of the Caffè Florian, once a meeting place for men of letters and travellers.

Following page Michele Marieschi, Piazza San Marco in Venice (detail). Private collection.

Pages 32–33 The Piazzetta of San Marco.

The Piazzetta

The **Libreria Sansoviniana** (Sansovino's Library) and the Doge's Palace face the Piazzetta. The classical facade of Jacopo Sansovino's masterpiece is crowned by a balustrade decorated with statues of mythological divinities.

It includes the **Biblioteca Marciana** which was established when, in 1468, Cardinal Bessarione left his collection of books to the Venetian Republic. The Marciana library is one of the most important collections in the world, and it houses more than 900,000 volumes, incunabola, and precious manuscripts.

Two tall granite columns stand at the quay end of the Piazza: on one is the Lion of St Mark, on the other, the statue of St. Theodore (Tòdaro), the first patron saint of Venice. Up until the end of the 18th century the execution of criminals took place between these two columns.

Above
*Libreria
Sansoviniana.*

*Detail of the
balustrade of the
Libreria
Sansoviniana
decorated with
mythological
divinities.*

*Manuscripts from
the Biblioteca
Marciana.*

*A reading room
in the Biblioteca
Marciana.*

*High water
in the Piazzetta
of San Marco.*

*Statue of
St. Theodore on
one of the columns
in the Piazzetta
of San Marco.*

*Francesco Guardi,
Piazzetta San
Marco facing San
Giorgio. Ca' d'Oro.*

Basilica of San Marco

The building that so majestically dominates the piazza is the Basilica of San Marco, framed by the two wings of the arcades and buildings of the Vecchie and Nuove Procuratie which open slightly, like a fan, to enhance the effect. The original basilica was built in the 9th century, and important restorations were made at the end of the 10th century. The actual building dates back to 1063 when it was rebuilt supposedly on the model of the Basilica of the Twelve Apostles in Constantinople. Since then, San Marco has been embellished throughout the years with artistic elements that have reflected the tastes of various periods. The church had been built in order to receive the body of St. Mark, brought here from Alexandria in Egypt. The evangelist's symbol of the winged lion became the symbol of the city as well, and St. Mark, its patron saint. The basilica was also the private chapel of the doge, being next to his residence at the Doge's Palace, as well as the site of state ceremonies inasmuch as the official ones of the Republic like the investiture of the doge were held there.

Following page
Facade of the Basilica of San Marco.

Sunset on the Bacino di San Marco.

36

The Exterior of the Basilica

The facade includes two superimposed orders of arches. On the lower part, there are five bays with double orders of columns receding toward the portals. The **portal of Sant'Alipio** is the first on the left; the only ancient (13th century) mosaic of the facade is in its lunette: *The Translation of the Body of St. Mark into the Church.* The other lunettes also recount the transfer of the body of St. Mark. In this lunette, however, one can see the facade of the ancient basilica with the four bronze horses already at the center. The four large lunettes in the upper part were decorated in the Seicento with mosaics depicting scenes from the life of Christ. In front of the large window in the center are copies of the four gilded bronze horses which by now have become symbols of the city. Brought to Venice from Constantinople during the Crusades, they confer the portal with the look of a triumphal arch. They are said to be from Roman times; the orginals are in the Museum of St. Mark. The doges witnessed the ceremonies taking place in the piazza from this balcony.

Basilica of San Marco: detail of one of the lunettes on the upper order of the facade.

The Tetrarchs, a sculptural group in porphyry between the Basilica and the Doge's Palace.

Basilica of San Marco: mosaic in the portal of Sant'Alipio.

The four horses of the Basilica of San Marco brought to Venice from Constantinople during the Fourth Crusade. Museo di San Marco.

The Narthex

Before entering the church itself, one enters the **narthex**, or atrium, which surrounds the sides of the church, and acts as a mediator between the noisy, open, outer space and the quiet inner religious space, bathed in golden light. The atrium mosaics, among the most beautiful in the basilica, narrate stories from the Old Testament.

The narthex mosaics, of the 13th century, scenes representing the *Creation of the World, Adam and Eve, Noah's Ark,* and the *Life of Joseph* are almost miniaturistic in character. The mosaics that are the most striking are those in the first cupola which depict twenty-four scenes from *Genesis* on three concentric bands.

Details of the narthex of the Basilica of San Marco.

Following page
An image of the splendid mosaics inside the Basilica.

Below left
Cupola of Genesis.

40

The interior of the church is in the form of a Greek cross with five domes covering the four arms and the center. The play of light and reflections on the sparkling mosaics create an awesome setting. Almost four thousand square meters of mosaics cover the walls, vaults and domes, revealing a typically Oriental taste in the decoration of the spacious gold grounds. In part original, 12th–14th centuries, in part modern, the subject of the mosaics is the glorification of Christ's Church and the Church of Venice and St. Mark. The mosaics are arranged on a Byzantine iconological scheme to accompany and complete the religious ceremonies which are being celebrated. The *Glorification of Christ's Church* is reprsented along the main axis of the church, *Christ Pantocrator* in the apse lunette, followed by the domes of *Christ Emmanuel*, the *Ascension*, and lastly, that of the *Pentecost*. the *Feasts of the Church* are represented on the sides. The *Stories of St. Mark* and the most popular *Saints of Venice* are narrated in the aisles.

Some of the most beautiful mosaics depicting the *Ascension* and dating to the 13th century, are in the central dome. *Christ Offering Benediction* and born into heaven by four angels is in the center, surrounding Him is the *Virgin between Two Angels and the Twelve Apostles*, and below them, between the windows, are sixteen seated female figures symbolizing the *Virtues* and *Beatitudes*.

Even the basilica floor is paved in marble mosaics which create an elaborate Oriental carpet with floral and geometric designs, wreaths, and polychrome borders.

The mosaics (13th century) of the interior of the basilica.

Opposite Stories of the Life of the Virgin and Scenes of the Passion.

Following page The mosaics of the dome of the Ascension.

The Pala d'Oro

Details of the Pala d'Oro inside the Basilica of San Marco.

T he most precious work of art in the basilica is above the main altar, the **Pala d'Oro** (Golden Altarpiece). This icon, almost three and a half meters long, was started in 976 A.D. and continued to be embellished up to the Trecento. It is an extremely elaborate piece of goldwork studded with precious stones and enamels. Two hundred and fifty enamelled squares enclosed in a gold-plated silver frame represent sacred subjects. According to an 18th-century inventory, there are 1300 pearls, 300 sapphires, 15 rubies and some 400 garnets.

Following pages The Pala d'Oro

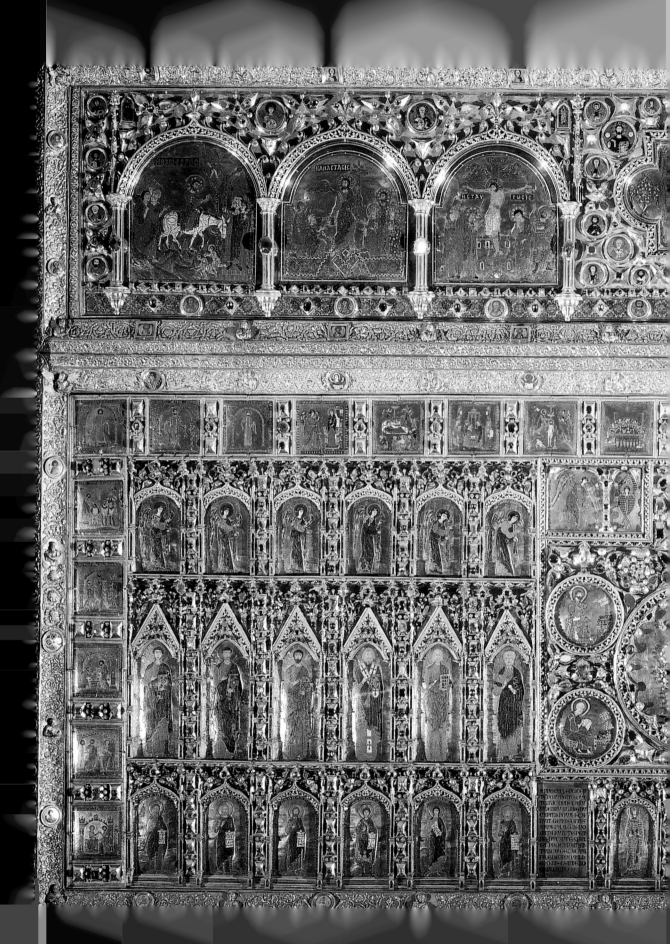

The Baptistry and Treasury of St. Mark

In the **Baptistry**, on the right of the church, is a vast area with three vaults. Above the walls the domes are covered with magnificent mosaics depicting episodes from the lives of Jesus and St. John the Baptist. In the center of the Baptistry is Jacopo Sansovino's baptismal font.

Of particular interest in the Baptistry is the mosaic in the lunette depicting *Salome's Dance*: the beautiful red gown of the cruel princess seems to be trimmed with ermine on the hem and sleeves.

The influence of contemporary Venetian painting is already discernable in these mid-14th century mosaics.

The **Treasury of St. Mark** was constituted in the 13th century and contains sacred objects and relics brought to Venice after the conquest of Constantinople. Sacked after the fall of the Republic, it still has a precious collection of silver and Byzantine gold objects.

Copies of the bronze horses have been placed on the facade of the basilica, while the originals are kept in the Museum of St. Mark.

The interior of the Baptistry: baptismal font by Jacopo Sansovino.

The Treasury of St. Mark.

Baptistry: Salome's Dance.

The Doge's Palace

Up until the fall of the Venetian Republic in 1797 the Doge's Palace was the residence of the doges and the most prestigious symbol of the political, cultural and military might of Venice. The palace housed the doge's private apartments, the armories and prisons, as well as the state apartments and the rooms where the ruling powers met. Historical evidence from many centuries is to be found inside the palace: the original ancient foundations, the Gothic structure in its entirety, the splendid paintings of the Venetian Renaissance painters, and the dark dank prisons Byron sang of in his poems. The Doge's Palace, as seen today, is itself the result of a series of restorations that occurred during the centuries whenever parts of it were destroyed by fire.

The Doge's Palace seen from the lagoon.

Following page Luca Carlevarijs, Arrival of the English Ambassador, Count of Manchester, at the Doge's Palace. Birmingham City Museum and Art Gallery.

50

The Exterior of the Doge's Palace

The exterior of the palace is one of the most impressive examples of Gothic architecture, and presents a daring reversal of equilibrium with a monolithic block on the upper floor supported by a graceful loggia and arcade on the ground floor running along the sides of the palace facing the lagoon and the Piazzetta. The ninth and tenth columns on the side closest to the Basilica mark the place where death sentences were read, while the thirteenth column is larger than the others because it indicates the end of the Chamber of the Great Council on the upper story.

The principal entrance to the palace was the **Porta della Carta,** designed by Giovanni and Bartolomeo Bon in the mid-15th century. It is believed that it was so named because it may have contained an archive or because scribes had their offices there. Above this majestic Gothic arcade is placed the statue of the doge Francesco Foscari kneeling before the lion of St. Mark.

Above
Porta della Carta, detail with the doge kneeling before the lion of St. Mark.

Opposite
Porta della Carta.

Loggia of the Doge's Palace seen from the Riva degli Schiavoni.

A charming image of the openwork tracery of the loggia.

Many of the splendid capitals decorating the arcade and the upper loggia of the Doge's Palace are copies of the originals, which are conserved inside in the museum of the palace. "The most beautiful capital in Europe," as the English writer John Ruskin defined capital no. 19, depicting *The Creation*, at the corner of the palace. *Adam and Eve* are represented on the corner of this 14th century capital which is attributed to Filippo Calendario, the original of which is in the Museo dell'Opera (the museum of the Doge's Palace).

An iconographic reading of the exterior facade of the Doge's Palace depicting the history of man and the universe can be made starting from this capital. The sujbects of the colonnade capitals are astrological, biblical and allegorical while those of the loggia are mostly decorative with floral motifs and human elements.

Outer corner of the Doge's Palace: Eve (full view and detail).

Above
One of the capitals of the Doge's Palace in the Museo dell'Opera.

Detail of a capital of the Doge's Palace.

DENONTIE SECRETE
CONTRO CHI OCCVLTERÃ
GRATIE ET OFFICII.
Õ COLLVDERÁ PER
NASCONDER LA VERA
RENDITA Ð ESSI.

The Museo dell'Opera

The museum is located on the ground floor of the Doge's Palace in an area that once housed prisons: the ancient wall is more than three feet wide and there is a column with a capital dating back to the 12th–13th centuries. The original capitals from the colonnade and the outer loggia, all except one from the 14th century, have been placed here. The forty original capitals were substituted by copies in the 19th century when the building underwent major renovations.

Doge's Palace: lion's mouth for secret denouncements.

The Museo dell'Opera in the Doge's Palace.

The Scala dei Giganti and the Scala d'Oro

In the courtyard of the Doge's Palace, which is as majestic as the rest, is a continuation of arches and loggias interrupted by the **Scala dei Giganti**, the late Cinquecento stairway used during ceremonies. Here the incoronation of the Doge took place, at which time he received the "zoia" or ducal beret from the eldest Councillor.

The name of the stairway comes from the two gigantic statues at its top: Neptune and Mars, symbols of the maritime and terrestrial power of the Serene Republic, which were sculpted by Jacopo Sansovino.

The **Scala d'Oro**, located on the loggia floor of the palace, derives its name from the gilded stuccoes of its vaulted ceiling. The stairway was reserved for very important people. Jacopo Sansovino's project was started in 1554 and finished four years later by Scarpagnino.

Beside the Scala d'Oro is a lion's mouth for secret denouncements. The accusations, both signed and anonymous, which were found in the different lion mouths throughout the palace generally gave rise to judicial proceedings.

Above
*Inner courtyard
of the Doge's Palace.*

Opposite
*The Scala
dei Giganti.*

Following page
The Scala d'Oro.

The Doge's Apartment

The **Doge's Apartment**, ten or so rooms in which the doge conducted his private life, has recently been reopened to the public. The rooms are decorated with period pieces and paintings by major artists of the Venetian School.

When a doge died his heirs were obliged to remove all of his furniture and belongings within three days, thus vacating the apartments before the next doge arrived.

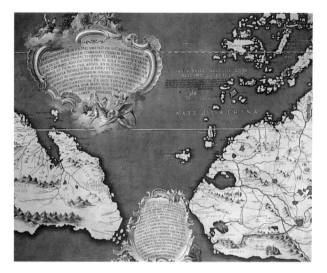

Top to bottom
Map of Asia and America in the Doge's Apartment.

The Doge's Apartment.

Giambattista Tiepolo, Neptune Offering Venice the Riches of the Sea. Sala delle Quattro Porte.

Left
Titian, St. Christopher. Sala dei Filosofi.

Paolo Veronese, The Triumph of Venice.

Sala del Maggior Consiglio and, in the background, Paradise by Jacopo Tintoretto and followers.

Sala del Maggior Consiglio and Sala dello Scrutinio

The monumental proportions of the **Sala del Maggior Consiglio** (Hall of the Great Council) make it the largest room in the palace. The Great Council, composed of nobles of at least twenty years of age, met here—in the Cinquecento it counted two thousand representatives—to approve laws and elect the high officials of the Serene Republic. The walls and ceiling of the salon are decorated with masters of Venetian painting such as Tintoretto and Veronese. On the upper part of walls are portraits of all the doges up to the Cinquecento; however, a black cloth marks the place of Marin Faliero, the doge who was decapitated for plotting against the state. At one time Guariento's fresco decorated the throne wall of the Sala del Maggior Consiglio. It was seriously damaged after a fire in 1577, and covered by Tintoretto's painting. Now the restored fresco is exhibitd in the Sala dell'Armamento.

The **Sala dello Scrutinio** in the 1500s was used for the scrutiny of the Great Council's voting. Here it is possible to see the restored ceiling paintings of Venice's victories over the other Maritime Republics.

Domenico Tintoretto, Portrait of Doge Marco Barbarigo.

Anticollegio and Collegio

The **Sala dell'Anticollegio**, the anteroom where delegations waited to be received by the doge, has a splendid fireplace and paintings of mythological subjects by Tintoretto and Veronese. The **Sala del Collegio**, was where the magistrates of the College received foreign delegations and decided on the agenda of the Senate of the Republic. Some of Veronese's most beautiful paintings are set into the gilded and inlaid wooden ceiling.

Sale del Collegio and Anticollegio.

Below
Paolo Veronese, Mars and Neptune; Venice with Peace and Justice. Sala del Collegio, ceiling.

Following page
Jacopo Tintoretto, The Marriage of St. Catherine. Sala del Collegio.

Sala del Senato and Sala del Consiglio dei Dieci

Padovanino,
Allegory of the War
with the Lega
Sacra. Sala
del Senato.

All political acts, foreign affairs, and declarations of war were decided in the **Sala del Senato**. The ceiling and wall paintings are yet another demonstration of Venice's prestige as are the decorations in the **Sala del Consiglio dei Dieci** (the Chamber of the Council of Ten) where decisions were taken regarding political crimes.

On the ceiling of the room there is a famous painting by Paolo Veronese: *Juno Offering the Doge's Cap, Gems and Gold to Venice.*

Following page
Paolo Veronese,
Juno Offering the
Doge's Cap, Gems
and Gold to Venice.
Sala del Consiglio
dei Dieci.

Jacopo and Domenico Tintoretto, Triumphal Exaltation of Venice. Sala del Senato.

Sala del Senato.

*Paolo Veronese, Aged
Oriental and Young Woman.
Sala del Consiglio dei Dieci.*

*Sala del Consiglio
dei Dieci.*

Sala della Bussola, the Armory, the Bridge of Sighs and the Piombi

The **Sala della Bussola** (Compass) was where criminals waited to learn their destiny; and the Armory, where a substantial number of weapons were deposited in the middle of the 1500s for use, not display. Prisoners awaiting trial crossed over the **Bridge of Sighs** from the New Prisons on the other side of the rio to the courts in the Doge's Palace.

The palace housed some other prisons as well: the **Piombi**, so-called because of their lead roofs. The 18th century Venetian adventurer Giacomo Casanova was imprisoned in the Piombi, from which, however, he managed to escape. Casanova himself gave a detailed description of the Piombi and his adventurous escape from them in his book, published in 1788, which was enormously successful throughout Europe.

Above
The Sala della Bussola and Casanova's prison in the Piombi.

Left
Hieronymus Bosch Santa Liberata Triptych (detail).

Right
Armour of Henri IV of France. Armory.

Following page
The Bridge of Sighs.

San Marco

The city of Venice is divided into six districts called "sestieri": San Marco, Castello and Cannaregio on one side of the Grand Canal; Dorsoduro, San Polo and Santa Croce on the other. Buildings are numbered progressively, not by street, but by sestiere. Therefore building numbers can reach four digits and, in some sestieri, number as high as six thousand. The sestiere of San Marco represents the heart of the city for it is the center of all political and commercial activity as well as being the location of the principal religious buildings. Tourists crowd this area more than any other, and the calli known as the "Mercerie" which join Piazza San Marco with the Rialto Bridge are filled with restaurants and all kinds of beautiful shops. A few steps from the Piazza is the world-renowned Harry's Bar, a luxurious bar and restaurant made famous and frequented by the American writer Ernest Hemingway.

The Palazzo Contarini, known especially for the Scala del Bovolo, a magnificent exterior spiral staircase which winds around a series of Venetian Gothic style loggias. (In Venetian dialect "bovolo" means "snail" or "spiral"). There is a wonderful view over the rooftops of the city from the top.

But there are other famous places to be found in this sestiere. Best known among classical music lovers and opera buffs is the Gran Teatro La Fenice, celebrated throughout the world for its remarkable acoustics, where renowned artists have played and sung. The theater was built in the late 18th century. In addition to its main entrance on Campo San Fantin, another one is located on the canal surrounding the theater where Venetian patricians once arrived in their gondolas.

The interior of Harry's Bar.

High water in Venice.

Scala del Bovolo.

Before the recent fire, the La Fenice could seat about eight hundred people. On the night of January 29, 1996 a terrible fire gutted the building, leaving only its facade and outer walls standing. The city administration of Venice has promised to reconstruct the theater as it was and where it was. La Fenice had already been destroyed by fire once before and rebuilt in 1836; it just so happens that the symbol of the theater is the phoenix, the legendary bird which dies but is always reborn from its own ashes.

The fire of La Fenice in 1996.

The symbol of La Fenice.

Interior of La Fenice.

Since the time of its greatest splendor, Venice has been a theater for spectacular events and sumptuous religious ceremonies throughout the year. Everything was celebrated—military victories, the visits of ambassadors and sovereigns, religious festivals—and the Doge, by his presence, honored these moments which constituted a veritable ritual in civic life. The fame of Venice's celebrations was such as to attract many foreigners to the city from Italy and the rest of Europe. Moreover, the relative autonomy that Venice enjoyed allowed for a certain freedom and tolerance in the entertainments held there. The queen of the festivals was, and still is, Carnival, which in the past started on December 26 and reached its culmination on Mardi Gras. During that time of year, the city turned into a huge stage where everything was permitted; social differences disappeared behind masks, and there were balls, festivities, and games in every corner of the city. The Carnival celebrations of the Settecento were the most spectacular of all, but recently masks and costumes have returned to regale Venice, albeit for a shorter period than in the past, during the ten days preceding Lent.

Gondolas and Carnival: a Venetian tradition.

Venetian masks.

Night on the Piazza San Marco: the natural conclusion to Venice's Carnival.

Below
Venetian masks are one of the most typical examples artisans' work of the city.

Performance in the Piazzetta in front of the Doge's Palace.

Masks

The use of masks has always been widespread in Venice, and the craftsmen who made them were once organized in a specific guild. The masks are made from papier-mâché. The most typical is the "baùta," a black or white mask that is slightly pointed and covers the face to just below the nose. It is usually worn with an ample black cape, the "tabarro," and a three-cornered hat.

69

Castello

The sestiere of Castello is the largest in the city extending from behind the Basilica of San Marco to Sant'Elena, the farthermost point of the city, facing the island of Lido. The Castello district is one of the richest in treasures to discover, some well-known, others less so. One of these is behind the Basilica of San Marco: the **Cloister of the Sant' Apollonia Convent**. This small but charming cloister dates back to the 12th–13th centuries and is Romanesque in style, something extremely unique in Venice.

The **Church of San Zaccaria**, with its imposing facade is the work of Mauro Codussi, one of the most important Venetian Renaissance architects.

Campo Santa Maria Formosa is one of the biggest squares in the city. Behind the church is **Palazzo Querini Stampalia**, the seat of the foundation of the same name. This unique example of a house-museum which conserves the entire patrimony of an ancient Venetian family includes the palace, the furnishings, a library, and an important collection of paintings by Palma il Vecchio, Tiepolo and Pietro Longhi among others.

Riva degli Schiavoni.

Above
*Facade of the
Church of San
Zaccaria.*

Above right
*Giovanni Bellini,
Sacra
Conversazione.
Church of San
Zaccaria.*

*Cloister of Santa
Apollonia convent.*

*One of the rooms in
Palazzo Querini
Stampalia.*

Scuola di San Giorgio degli Schiavoni

The **Scuola di San Giorgio degli Schiavoni** is the site of a celebrated series of paintings by Vittore Carpaccio which mark the highest point of the artist's production.

Evidence of the cosmopolitan spirit of Venice is to be found in the names of the streets which often refer to foreign communities: the "Schiavoni" were Dalmatians; the "Ragusei" came from Ragusa, today's Dubrovnik; there were also the Albanians, the Greeks, the Armenians, a large community of Jews, all who lived in the ghetto.

Vittore Carpaccio, Cycle of the Scuola di San Giorgio degli Schiavoni. (from above) *St. Jerome Leads the Lion into the Monastery; St. George Baptizing the People of Silene; Funeral of St. Jerome.*

Following page *St. Augustine's Vision (detail).*

CALLE
DEI ALBANESI

S. ZACCARIA
PONTE
DEI GRECI

DE LA PIETÀ
RIVA DEGLI
SCHIAVONI

*Street names
referring
to foreign
communities.*

*San Giorgio
degli Schiavoni.*

Santi Giovanni e Paolo

The **Basilica of Santi Giovanni e Paolo**, one of the Castello district's most important buildings and a major example of sacred Gothic architecture, situated on the campo of the same name. The church was of great political and religious importance for the funerals of the doges and those of the Venetian heroes were held here starting in the early 1500s. Inside Santi Giovanni e Paolo are the tombs of the doges of the Venetian Republic. The church has masterpieces such as the rare stained glass window that decorates

the right transept, the *San Vincenzo Polyptych* by Giovanni Bellini and paintings by Paolo Veronese in the Cappella del Rosario. To the left of the Church of Santi Giovanni e Paolo is the Scuola Grande di San Marco; now the City Hospital of Venice.

The bronze equestrian **statue of the condottiero Bartolomeo Colleoni**, a Quattrocento masterpiece of the Florentine sculptor Andrea Verrocchio, dominates the "campo" in front of the church. Bartolomeo Colleoni, captain of adventure in the service of the Republic of Venice, promised to leave his fortune to the city on the understanding that a monument would be raised to him in Piazza San Marco. Since it was impossible to do so in that piazza, the Senate chose this campo which was equally prestigious and significant for the city.

Left
Funerary monument to Doge Nicolò Marcello. Basilica of Santi Giovanni e Paolo.

Above
Facade of the Basilica of Santi Giovanni e Paolo.

Below left
Andrea Verrocchio, Statue of Bartolomeo Colleoni, Campo of Santi Giovanni e Paolo.

Below right
Gentile Bellini, Portrait of Doge Giovanni Mocenigo. Museo Correr.

San Pietro in Castello

The **Church of San Pietro in Castello**, of ancient origin, was the cathedral of Venice until 1807 when the title passed to the Basilica of San Marco. The "campo" in front of the church is the only one in the city that is still grassy. Once all the open spaces in the city were which explains why the word "campo" (field) is used instead of "piazza."

Inside the Church of San Pietro in Castello is the so-called chair of St. Peter, a marble throne from Antioch which, according to legend, was used by the apostle.

St. Peter's chair in the Church of San Pietro in Castello.

Church of San Pietro in Castello.

The Arsenal

What really characterizes the sestiere of Castello is the **Arsenal**, a great complex of dockyards and workshops that was once the heart of Venice's naval power. The galleys of the Venetian fleet were built here, and later on, merchant ships and warships. The Venetian Arsenal dates far back in the past. It was already in existence in the Trecento when the poet Dante Alighieri mentioned it in his *Divine Comedy*. The remains of the first Arsenal, used as a depot for weapons and naval equipment, date back to 1100. After 1320 it took on a more organic form and quadrupled in size, becoming a proper shipyard where vessels were not simply maintained but also built. In the middle of the 16th century the Arsenal employed some two to three thousand men, making it the biggest factory in the Christian world. Thanks to a system that is reminiscent of today's assembly line, the Arsenal managed to produce up to 100 galleys in two months' time. Today the only thing that remains of the Arsenal is its history and some traces of its architecture— the entrance gateway and the outer walls—and some buildings whose names at times recall its ancient splendor: the Arsenale Vecchio, the Arsenale Nuovo, and the Novissimo, the Vele, the Bucintoro (for the doge's boat was kept here), Le Corderie, etc. Le Corderie of the Arsenal, where cordage was made and stored, is one of the few places that is still visible and is often used as an exhibition space. The magnificent portal of the land entrance is considered the first Renaissance work in Venice. There are two huge marble lions on either side of the door. The lions were brought here from Athens' port of Piraeus as spoils of war by Admiral Francesco Morosini at the end of the 17th century.

One of the lions of the entrance to the Arsenal.
Arsenal: land entrance.

Following page
The Museum of Naval History next

door to the Arsenal conserves different models of Venetian boats incuding the most recent Bucintoro.

The Darsena Vecchia.

The Gardens of the Biennale

Almost at the tip of Venice are the public gardens, commonly called the **Gardens of the Biennale** because the pavilions of the Biennale of Contemporary Art, held every two years since 1895, are situated here. The art exhibition was originally open only to Italian artists but when the second exhibition was held it was decided to admit foreigners as well. This initiative was so successful that many countries decided to create permanent structures in order to exhibit their artists' works.

Many pavilions were designed by outstanding architects: the Venezuelan pavilion was built by the Italian Carlo Scarpa, Alvar Aalto designed the Finnish pavilion, and Josef Hoffman that of Austria.

Above
*Le Corderie
of the Arsenal.*

Right
*The Gardens
of the Biennale.*

Cannaregio

One of the largest and most populated districts of the city is the sestiere of Cannaregio. During the last century it was divided in two by the long "Strada Nova" that leads from the Railway Station, where the sestiere begins, and terminates not far from the Rialto Bridge. Cannaregio is still one of the most authentic areas of the city with its traditional wine bars where one can stop to drink an "ombra," a glass of wine and eat a "cichéto," a morsel of fish or polenta and codfish or some other local speciality. Many of the artisans work in this part of the city as they have for centuries, weaving precious damasks and other fabrics or sewing theatrical costumes.

The Church of Santa Maria dei Miracoli is a veritable Renaissance jewel, its facade and interior covered in polychrome marbles. Near the church is located one of the most important Gothic buildings in Venice, **Palazzo Van Axel**, which has two entrances, one on water and one on land. Its land entrance still conserves its original wooden 15th century doors complete with peephole.

Palazzo van Axel.

Church of Santa Maria dei Miracoli.

Ponte delle Guglie.   *A typical tavern
in Cannaregio.*

*The Nicolao
theatrical costume
atelier.*   *Loom for weaving
damasks.*

The Jewish Ghetto

One of the most beautiful and fascinating corners of Venice to visit is in Cannaregio: the **Jewish Ghetto**. Here, unlike elsewhere in the city, the houses are very tall, reaching eight stories at times: they are the so-called house-towers. This is due to the fact that when the Jewish population was confined here at the beginning of the 16th century, their numbers increased so rapidly that the only solution was to build additional floors. There are still five synagogues in the Ghetto of which three can be visited. They were all built between the 16th and 17th centuries and important Italian architects collaborated in their construction. The German synagogue which was built in 1528 is the oldest. The largest is the Spanish synagogue which originally dates back to the middle of the 16th century but was rebuilt in the following century when the great architect Baldassarre Longhena almost cetainly worked on its facade.

Additional evidence of Jewish art and culture is exhibited in the Jewish Museum, in the Campo of the Ghetto Nuovo, which houses a collection of sacred objects, silver and codices from the 17th to the 19th centuries.

The Venetian ghetto is the oldest in the world: the term "ghetto" may originate from the Venetian "getàr," to fuse, because there were many foundries in this area. Signs of the presence of the Jewish community, confined here since 1516, are still to be found. One example are the holes in the entrance gates of the Ghetto Vecchio and the Ghetto Novo, where bars were inserted at night to keep the Jews inside the ghetto.

Characteristic house-towers, the skyscrapers of the period.

Campo of the Ghetto Novo.

Holes in the
entrance gates
to the Ghetto
Vecchio.

German synagogue
in the Campo of the
Ghetto Novo.

The Spanish
synagogue.

Campo dei Mori

The **Campo dei Mori** is located in one of the city's quieter areas and less crowded with tourists; it takes its name from the 13th century stone figures inserted in the lateral wall of Palazzo Mastelli or "del Cammello." According to tradition, the statues in the Campo dei Mori are those of the owners of this palace, rich merchants from the Morea. The palazzo is also called "del Cammello" because of the high-relief depicting a camel to the right of the balcony. Next to the Campo dei Mori is the **house of Jacopo Tintoretto**, and

behind it, his parish church, the **Church of the Madonna dell'Orto,** for which the great 16th-century artist painted a magnificent cycle of works in the interior.

Above right
and following page
*Church of the
Madonna dell'Orto,
one of the most
interesting
examples of
Venetian Gothic.*

*Palazzo Mastelli
or "del Cammello"
and (above left)
detail of the facade.*

Above
*A statue in the
Campo dei Mori.*

Dorsoduro

The sestiere of Dorsoduro extends from the Punta della Dogana, which faces the Bacino di San Marco and separates the Grand Canal from the Giudecca Canal, to the Maritime Station. It is considered one of the more chic residential areas of the city, and also one of the most beautiful. This is primarily because of the lovely walk called **"Le Zattere"** that runs along the Giudecca Canal from the Punta della Dogana to the port. To meet for a walk along the Zattere, which faces south and is therefore very sunny, is a favorite pastime for tourists and Venetians alike. Even in the coldest months of winter when the sun is shining it is possible to eat outdoors or enjoy the best ice cream in the city .

The **Squero di San Trovaso** is not far from the Gallerie dell'Accademia. It is an interesting place to visit since it is one of the few boatyards still operating in Venice; gondolas are built here. The houses surrounding the Squero resemble those on Mount Cadore, which is where the wood used for building the gondolas came from. The 15th-century Squero of San Trovaso is thought to be the oldest in Venice.

The **Campo Santa Margherita** is another of the city's large open spaces and filled with coffee bars and night spots. It is particularly popular with young people because of its proximity to the university institutes. However, on the edge of this sestiere is one of Venice's least known, but most beautiful treasures, the **Church of San Sebastiano**. Small and hidden away in the outskirts of the city, it is a monument to Paolo Veronese's paintings. The artist had free reign when he decorated the ceiling, vaults, walls, apse, sacristy, and friars' choir with frescoes, creating his typical effects of optical illusions.

The Basilica della Salute.

*Church of
San Sebastiano.*

Above, right
*The Fondamenta
delle Zattere with
the Church of the
Redentore in the
background.*

*The Squero di San
Trovaso.*

*Fruit stand
on the barge near
the Campo San
Barnaba.*

*Campo Santa
Margherita.*

GALLERIE DELL'ACCADEMIA

The Gallerie dell'Accademia, one of the most important museums of the world, possess works of inestimable value from the Trecento to the end of the Settecento, and is unique in that all the works are of the same school: the Venetian School. In this relatively small museum, which can only exhibit part of its immense patrimony due to lack of space, are gathered the Trecento Byzantine and Gothic works of Paolo Veneziano, the early Renaissance paintings of Carpaccio and Bellini, and those of the Cinquecento ranging from Giorgione and Titian to Tintoretto and Veronese, up through the Settecento works of Ricci, Longhi, Canaletto, Guardi, and many others. The collection includes such masterpieces as *Feast in the House of Levi*, the enormous canvas by Paolo Caliari, called Veronese, originally meant to represent the *Last Supper*. The Inquisition tribunal maintained that the figures painted in it were not suitable for a sacred subject—the buffoon holding a parrot, a man cleaning his teeth with a toothpick, another whose nose is bleeding—and so Veronese changed its title to the one it still bears.

One of the exhibition rooms in the Gallerie dell'Accademia.

*Giorgione,
The Tempest.*

*Paolo Veronese,
Feast in the House
of Levi.*

*Giovanni Bellini,
Allegory to
"Inconstant
Fortune."*

VENETIAN PAINTING

Venetian painting developed as an ideal continuation of the Byzantine tradition. The mosaics in the Basilica of San Marco already showed a particular use of color that would later become the main characteristic of Venetian art. The Byzantine influence was still evident in the Trecento paintings of Paolo Veneziano with their gold grounds and eastern motifs, however, the richness of color was already striking. Giovanni Bellini renewed this art by inserting his figures into architectural spaces and by introducing landscape motifs. Carpaccio left his mark with the narrative cycles like the *Legend of Saint Ursula* at the Gallerie dell'Accademia or the *Stories of Saint George* at the Scuola di San Giorgio degli Schiavoni. Giorgione endowed his canvases with a transparent luminosity thanks to the pictorial technique he perfected. An inceasingly expressive use of light and color was transmitted in Titian's masterpieces, and then transformed into the dramatic chiaroscuro tones of Tintoretto's works and later into the luminous settings of Veronese and Tiepolo.

Giovanni Bellini, Madonna and Child Between Sts.Catherine and Mary Magdalene (detail).Gallerie del'Accademia.

Lorenzo Lotto, Young Man in His Study. Gallerie dell'Accademia.

Above right *Titian, Pietà. Gallerie dell'Accademia.*

Following page *Titian, Presentation of the Virgin in the Temple (full view and detail). Gallerie dell'Accademia.*

Near Campo San Barnaba is the beautiful **Ca' Rezzonico**. It houses the Museum of the Venetian Settecento and is also a venue for temporary exhibitions. Recently restored, this elegant 18th-century residence is decorated with period furnishings in all of its rooms together with paintings by Longhi, Canaletto and Guardi. The ceilings of many of the rooms were frescoed by Giambattista Tiepolo, many of whose most important works are to be found in this palace, namely, the *Nuptial Allegory*, and the *Allegory of the Merit Between Nobility and Virtue* in the Throne Room.

The facade of
Ca' Rezzonico.

Two rooms
of Ca' Rezzonico.

Right
*Pietro Longhi, The
Family Concert.*

Left
*Pietro Longhi, The
Parlatory of Nuns.*

Opposite
*Giambattista
Tiepolo, The
Triumph of Zephyr
and Flora (detail).
Ca'Rezzonico.*

The Giudecca

The **Giudecca** is the biggest island and the closest to Venice. Its name originates either from Giudei, the Jews, who may have once been confined there or from the word *zudegà*, judged, which refers to the rebellious noble families who had been banned from the city and exiled to the island. The Giudecca has many interesting architectural works, in particular, the two churches designed by Andrea Palladio. Right in front of the Bacino di San Marco, set between the two wings of the convent, is Santa Maria della Presentazione, which is usually called the **Church of the Zitelle** (Spinsters) for the poor girls who were given shelter there. Construction of the whole complex, including church, hospice and cloister, started in 1570 on designs by Palladio. Nearby is the magnificent **Basilica del Redentore**, one of the most splendid examples of church architecture by Andrea Palladio, built to give thanks for the city's deliverance from the plague in 1576. The scenographic and celebrative effect created here is deliberate: the façade rises above a solemn stairway, the basilica is crowned by a huge dome and flanked by two small lateral bell towers. The luminous interior has one nave, and contains paintings by Francesco Bassano and Palma il Giovane.

At the western extremity of the Giudecca is a huge industrial complex, now abandoned: the **Mulino Stucky**. The construction of the Mulino Stucky in neo-Gothic style at the end of the last century by the German architect Ernest Wullekopf created consternation throughout the city because of its lofty style and the way it imposed, and still does, on the Venetian skyline.

Above
*Island of
the Giudecca.*

Opposite
Mulino Stucky.

Following page
*The Basilica
del Redentore
on the Giudecca.*

THE FEAST OF THE REDEEMER

Among the religious holidays celebrated in Venice, the best known is the **Feast of the Redeemer**, which has been celebrated for more than four hundred years on the third Saturday and Sunday of July. On this occasion, the Venetians commemorate the city's deliverance from the plague in 1576 at which time Andrea Palladio was commissioned to build the Basilica del Redentore (Redeemer) on the island of the Giudecca in order to give thanks. On Sunday, as in the time of the doges, the religious and civic authorities lead a procession over a bridge of boats that is built every year from the Fondamenta delle Zattere to the front of the Basilica. However, the Saturday night festivity is more evocative because it has maintained its popular character throughout the years. At sunset, all kinds of boats, decorated with boughs, lanterns and festoons, gather around the floating pontoons in the Bacino di San Marco where magnificent fireworks are set off at midnight.

Joseph Heintz,
The Bridge of the
Redentore. Museo
Correr.

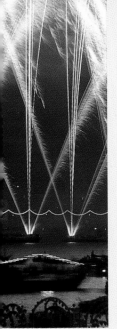

Fireworks and decorated boats during the Feast of the Redeemer.

San Polo and Santa Croce

The sestieri of San Polo and Santa Croce include that part of the city that extends from the Rialto Bridge to the automobile terminal at Piazzale Roma. The big markets at the foot of the Rialto Bridge, which have always been located there, are the heart of San Polo and the commercial hub of the city.

Indeed, the Rialto Bridge was made as high as it is so that the galleys coming from the Bacino di San Marco and carrying their loads up the Grand Canal could pass under it. Half-hidden by the fruit barrows at the foot of the bridge is the Church of **San Giacometto**, the only one to have survived the great fire of 1514 that razed everything to the ground. The church, the oldest in the city according to tradition, has a big Quattrocento clock on its facade. A Latin inscription on the apse outside ties the church to the commercial activities going on around it for it reminds merchants to be honest, exact in weighing, and loyal in contracting. The "Hunchback of the Rialto," the statue in front of the church of San Giacometto, holds up the ladder of the Colonna del Bando (Proclamation Column), from which laws and sentences were proclaimed.

Facade of the Church of San Giacometto.

Rialto fruit and vegetable market.

Rialto fish market.

Rialto fish market (detail).

Santa Maria Gloriosa dei Frari

The Church of **Santa Maria Gloriosa dei Frari**, the second largest monumental complex after that of Piazza San Marco, is the huge and magnificent building that, together with the Basilica di Santi Giovanni e Paolo, represents the greatest examples of Venetian Gothic religious architecture. Started in the Trecento, it was completed almost one century later. The soaring brick facade is decorated with a series of niches and a clever combination of arches and pilasters. The interior is so rich in works of art that it resembles a museum more than a church. The most beautiful work without a doubt is Titian's *Assumption* which immediately stands out to those who, upon passing through the main entrance, see it framed by the arch leading to the wooden choir stalls. The latter are among the most marvellous treasures of the church: three tiers of seats with 124 stalls decorated with scenes from the lives of saints and Venetian life. The *Pesaro Altarpiece*, set on the family altar, is another masterpiece by Titian and should not be missed; also, a funerary monument to Antonio Canova, which had originally been designed by the sculptor for Titian; and, in the sacristy, a splendid triptych by Giovanni Bellini depicting the *Madonna Enthroned with Child and Saints*.

Above
Titian, The Assumption. Chiesa dei Frari.

Opposite
Titian, the Pesaro Altarpiece. Chiesa dei Frari.

Following page
Monumental complex of the Chiesa dei Frari.

Scuola Grande di San Rocco

The **Scuola Grande di San Rocco** is celebrated because it conserves the entire cycle of more than fifty paintings by Jacopo Tintoretto. San Rocco was one of the many devotional schools present in Venice; these lay confraternities dedicated to the veneration of a saint had spiritual, social, and charitable functions. Since wealthy people were included in their ranks, the Scuole were often decorated by the best artists of the times.

The imposing Scuola Grande di San Rocco was built at the beginning of the 16th century and even though several architects had their hand in its construction, the harmony of its volumes was maintained. The building includes two great halls, on the first and second floors and the Sala dell'Albergo, also on the second floor.

When a competition was announced for the decoration of the Sala dell' Albergo, all of the great painters in Venice participated, but as they presented their sketches, Tintoretto showed that he had already painted and installed the central panel. This was received so successfully that he was commissioned to do the rest of the Scuola.

Tintoretto also painted an enormous *Crucifixion* for the Sala dell'Albergo which was about twelve meters long and one of the few works that the artist signed (1565). He painted several scenes from the Old and New Testaments for the Salone Maggior upstairs, while the eight large canvases that decorate the ground-floor room were among the last he executed for the Scuola and date back to the last decade of his artistic activity.

Scuola Grande di San Rocco.

Jacopo Tintoretto, The Brazen Serpent. Ceiling of the Sala dell'Albergo, Scuola di San Rocco.

Jacopo Tintoretto, Crucifixion. Painted for the Sala dell'Albergo of the Scuola di San Rocco.

Jacopo Tintoretto,
The Annunciation.
Painted for the first
floor of the Scuola
di San Rocco.

Scuola Grande di San Giovanni Evangelista

The **Scuola Grande di San Giovanni Evangelista** is another important devotional school. It has an extremely scenographic entrance above which is the sculpture of an eagle, the symbol of St. John the Evangelist. The Scuola houses an important relic of the Holy Cross. This is kept in a precious silver and rock crystal Cross, a masterpiece of Venetian Gothic goldsmith's work, which is is to be found in the Oratory. The paintings of *The Miracles of the Cross* by Gentile Bellini and Vittore Carpaccio which once decorated the room are now in the Gallerie dell'Accademia.

A monumental stairway characterizes the Scuola architecturally: it was built by Mauro Codussi in order to embellish the preexisting edifice and at the same time honor and glorify the reliquary it housed.

Scuola Grande di San Giovanni Evangelista.

The house where playwright Carlo Goldoni was born in 1707, with its charming courtyard and open Gothic stairway, is now also a center for theatrical studies. Carlo Goldoni wrote more than 250 plays and made such Commedia dell'Arte characters as Harlequin, Pulcinella, and Colombina famous.

His plays are still frequently presented in Venetian dialect in the "campi" and "campielli" of the city.

Alessandro Longhi, Portrait of Carlo Goldoni. Ca' Rezzonico.

The facade of Goldoni's house.

Interior of Goldoni's house.

103

The Lagoon

There are more than forty islands in the Venetian lagoon. By now some of these are completely abandoned and the buildings on them reduced to ruins; others are inhabited by just a few people; and still others are famous for what they produce. In addition to the more important islands discussed in the following pages, others are certainly well worth a visit.

In front of the island of Burano, on the opposite side from that facing Torcello, is the island of **San Francesco del Deserto** which has a monastery and a lovely garden overlooking the lagoon. According to legend, St. Francis landed here in 1220 on his way back from the Holy Land.

Between the Bacino of San Marco and the island of the Lido is one of the more interesting islands to visit: **San Lazzaro degli Armeni**. Like San Francesco del Deserto it still has a religious function. The Monastery of the Mekhitarist Fathers—with its splendid church, cloister and a library rich in manuscipts and miniatures dating back to the 9th century—is located in this place of rare beauty.

The **Lido** is situated on one of the long, narrow strips of land that divides the Venetian lagoon from the open sea. The island developed rapidly as an international resort at the beginning of this century when two hotels, the Grand Hotels Des Bains and the Excelsior Palace, were built there. The German writer Thomas Mann contributed to the fame of the place by making it the setting for his book *Death in Venice* (1912) which Luchino Visconti later made into a film. In the thirties the Lido became the venue for the International Film Festival which is still held every summer at the end of August.

Above
*Cloister of San
Lazzaro degli
Armeni* (left) *and
San Francesco
del Deserto* (right).

*Two images
of the lagoon.*

*San Lazzaro degli
Armeni: the room
where Lord Byron
was often a guest.*

*The Lido:
Palazzo del Cinema.*

Murano

Murano is known all over the world as "the island of glass." Its composition is much like that of Venice: a group of islands around a grand canal connected by bridges. Murano is also home to a 12th century Romanesque jewel, the **Church of Santi Maria e Donato**. The most original part of the church is its apse which faces the Canal of San Donato, an important "road" for pilgrims in the Middle Ages and for merchants landing from their ships. The apse, composed of a series of arches, niches, columns and marble inserts, contrasts with the rest of the building which is in red brick with a simple facade.

Church of Santi Maria e Donato.

The glass industry was once located in the center of Venice, but in 1291 after yet another terrible fire caused by the high temperatures required for baking the glass in the furnaces, the glassmakers were ordered to move out of the city. Those who had small furnaces were allowed to remain as long as their furnaces were five paces from any neighboring house. Therefore, the glassmakers moved to Murano which was isolated, yet not too far from Rialto, the center of traffic and commercial activity. The glassmakers' guild was very strong and enjoyed special privileges since the glass industry provided a lucrative source of income for Venice. The daughters of the master glassmakers, for instance, were permitted to marry into the noble families.

There are many important glassworks in Murano and many of the furnaces offer free demonstrations of glassmaking to the public. The **Museo d'Arte Vetraria** (Museum of the Art of Glassmaking) is worth a visit. It possesses a rich collection of objects, including the famous Barovier Cup, a 15th century wedding cup.

Two interesting moments of the glassmaking process.

Objects from the Museo d'Arte Vetraria di Murano.

Left:
Filigree pitcher "a reticello" from the 16th century.

Right
Glass vase, designed by Napoleone Martinuzzi, produced by Venini & C., 1926–30.

107

Burano

Burano is without a doubt the most picturesque island in the lagoon. Although it has no important architectural works, it is still worth visiting just to see its brightly-colored houses and lively fish market, and to watch how lace is made and taste the wonderful Burano pastries. Legend has it that the houses on Burano have always been painted in such bright colors so that the fishermen would be able to pick out their own when they came home on the foggy days of autumn. The houses are still painted every year and the different colors distinguish the different properties.

The island's characteristic way of making lace with a sewing needle had already developed by the early 16th century and soon became famous throughout Europe, especially because of the invention of the delicate "punto in aria." Today, real Burano lace is a luxury that few can afford. Just think: it takes ten lacemakers more than a year to make a tablecloth.

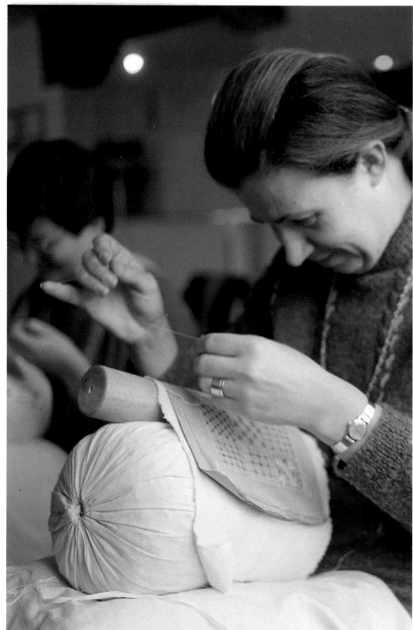

Above
The brightly-colored houses of Burano.

The art of lacemaking typical of Burano.

Torcello

When one leaves noisy, lively, and brightly-colored Burano and comes to this island of Torcello with less than fifty inhabitants, one is struck by the silence and peace that reign here. Yet it was once one of the most important islands in the lagoon, and among the first to be founded in the 5th century by the inhabitants of Altino, who lived further north on the mainland but had to flee from the invasion of the Huns. The **Cathedral of Santa Maria Assunta**, the remains of the **Baptistry** and the **Church of Santa Fosca** bear witness to the ancient splendor of the island. There is an inscription inside the Cathedral dated 639, making it the oldest Venetian monument, even though it was partially rebuilt around the year 1000. The remains of the original pavement which are much lower than the actual floor can be seen under a trap door. The inside facade wall has an enormous 12th-century mosaic depicting *The Last Judgment*. The work, which should be read from the top to the bottom, is divided into six episodes starting from the Crucifixion and ending in Limbo where the elected are separated from the damned.

In the garden is the so-called **Throne of Attila**, king of the Huns. It is much more likely that this marble seat was used by the tribunes who rendered justice in ancient times. Next to the monumental complex is the Locanda Cipriani, now only a restaurant, but famous for having had kings and queens and heads of states among its guests. In 1948 Ernest Hemingway retired here to write some chapters of his novel *Across the River and Into the Trees*.

The Devil's Bridge: on the canal that connects the monumental area with the lagoon is a bridge without parapets, as all Venetian bridges once were, which people say was built in just one night.

Torcello: interior of the Cathedral.

Torcello: Devil's Bridge.

Below
Torcello: Santa Fosca.

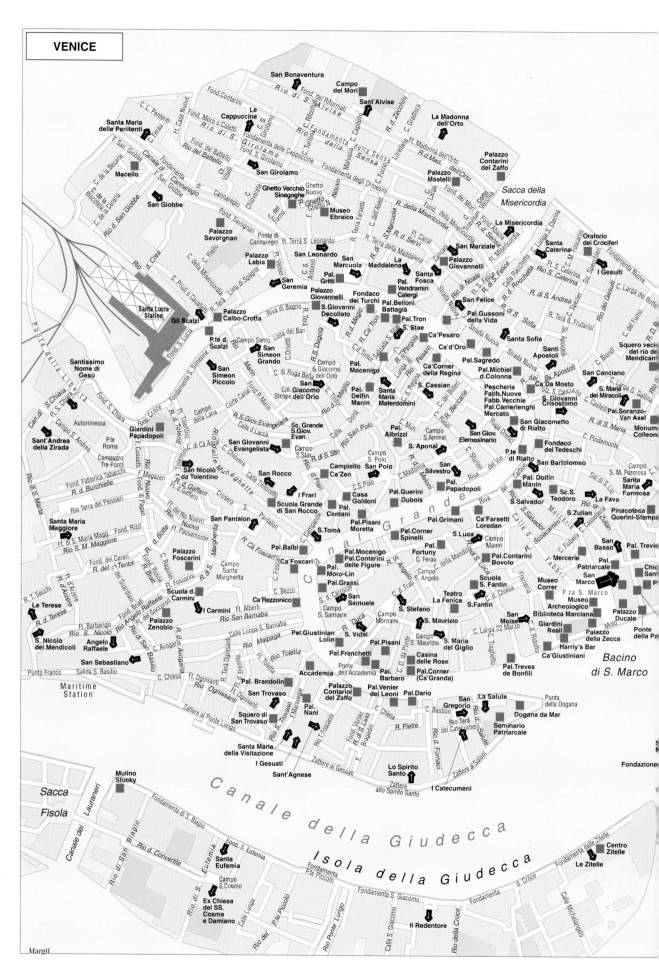

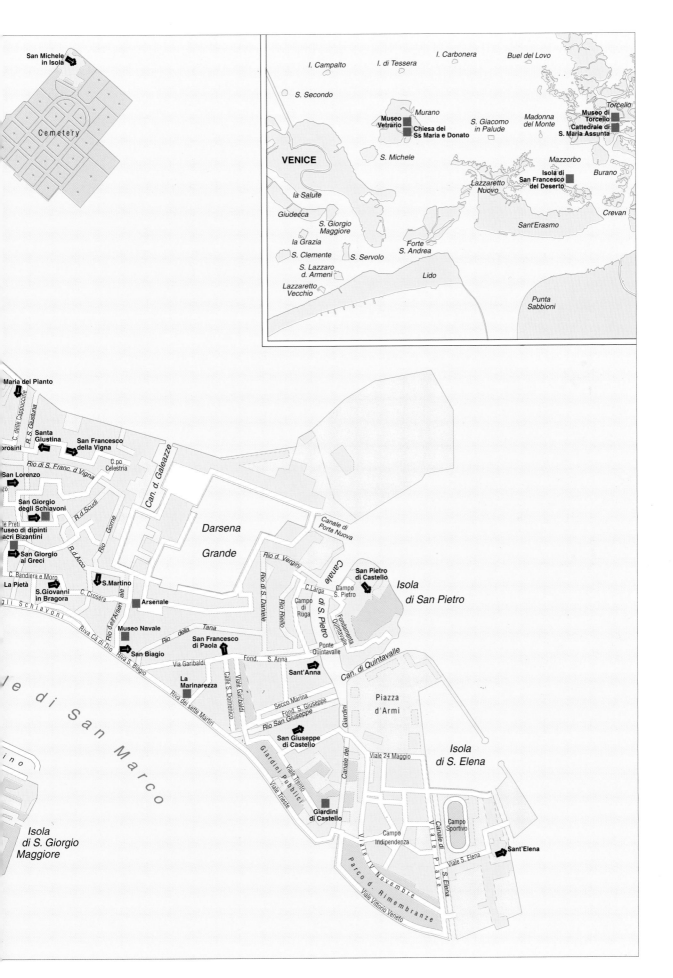

San Michele
in Isola

Cemetery

I. Campalto

I. di Tessera

I. Carbonera

Buel del Lovo

S. Secondo

Murano

Museo
Vetrario

Chiesa dei
Ss Maria e Donato

S. Giacomo
in Palude

Madonna
del Monte

Torcello

Museo di
Torcello

Cattedrale di
S. Maria Assunta

S. Michele

Mazzorbo

Burano

Lazzaretto
Nuovo

Isola di
San Francesco
del Deserto

Crevan

la Salute

Giudecca

S. Giorgio
Maggiore

Sant'Erasmo

la Grazia

S. Clemente

S. Servolo

Forte
S. Andrea

S. Lazzaro
d. Armeni

Lido

Lazzaretto
Vecchio

Punta
Sabbioni

Maria del Pianto

C. delle Cappuccine

R. S. Giustina

Santa
Giustina

San Francesco
della Vigna

orosini

Rio di S. Franc. d Vigna

C.po
Celestria

San Lorenzo

zo

San Giorgio
degli Schiavoni

R. d Scudi

Rio Gorne

Can. d. Galeazze

Darsena

Grande

Canale di
Porta Nuova

le Preti

Museo di dipinti
acri Bizantini

San Giorgio
ai Greci

R. d Arco

Rio d. Vergini

Rio d. S. Daniele

Rio Rielto

Canale di S. Pietro

San Pietro
di Castello

Isola
di San Pietro

C. Bandiera e Moro

La Pietà

S. Martino

C. Crosera

Arsenale

C. Larga

Campo
S. Pietro

Campo
di
Ruga

Fondamenta
Quintavalle

gli Schiavoni

Riva Cà di Dio

Rio del Arsen ale

Museo Navale

Rio della

Tana

San Francesco
di Paola

Ponte
Quintavalle

San Biagio

Riva S. Biagio

Via Garibaldi

Fond. S. Anna

Sant'Anna

Can. di Quintavalle

Riva dei sette Martiri

La Marinarezza

Calle S. Domenico

Viale Garibaldi

Secco Marina

Fond. S. Giuseppe

Rio San Giuseppe

Giardini

Piazza
d'Armi

Isola
di S. Elena

ino

Isola
di S. Giorgio
Maggiore

Giardini Pubblici

Viale Trento

Viale Trieste

San Giuseppe
di Castello

Viale 24 Maggio

Canale del

Campo
Sportivo

Giardini
di Castello

Campo
Indipendenza

Campo

Viale S. Elena

Canale di S. Elena

Viale Piave

Sant'Elena

Parco d. Rimembranze

Viale IV Novembre

Viale Vittorio Veneto

le di San Marco

Photograph Credits
Graziano Arici, Venice
Osvaldo Böhm, Venice
Cameraphoto, Venice
Electa Archive, Milan
Scala Archive, Florence

Translation
Rhoda Billingsley

This volume was printed by Elemond S.p.a.
at the plant in Martellago (Venice) in 1997.